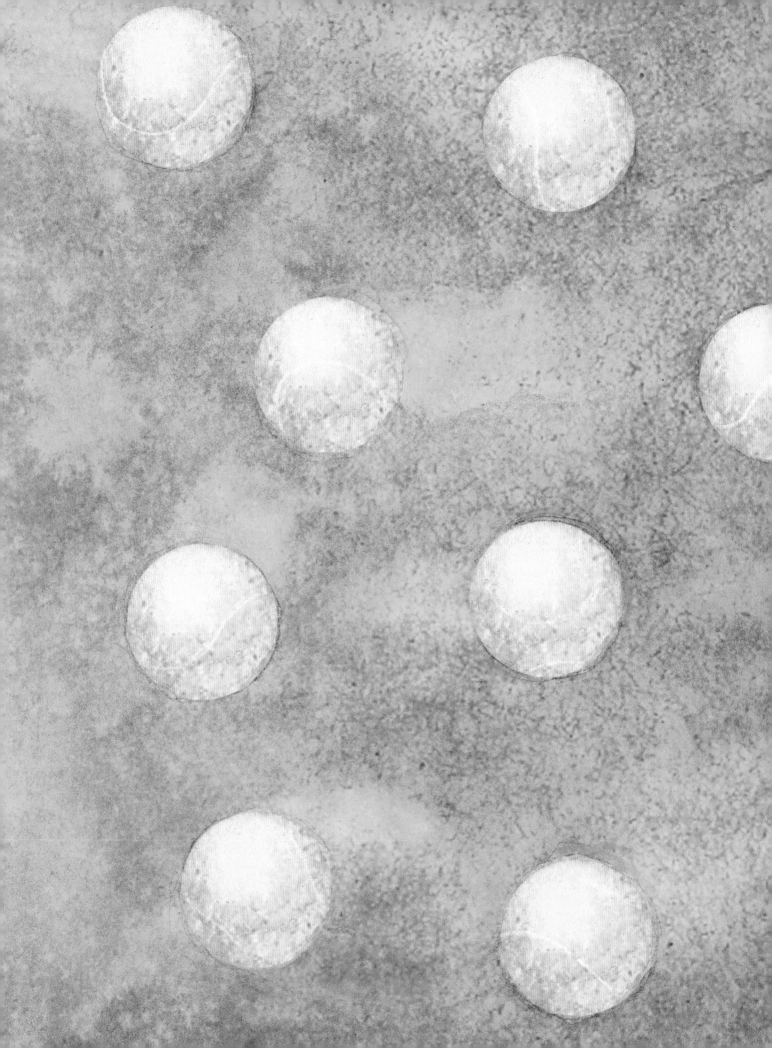

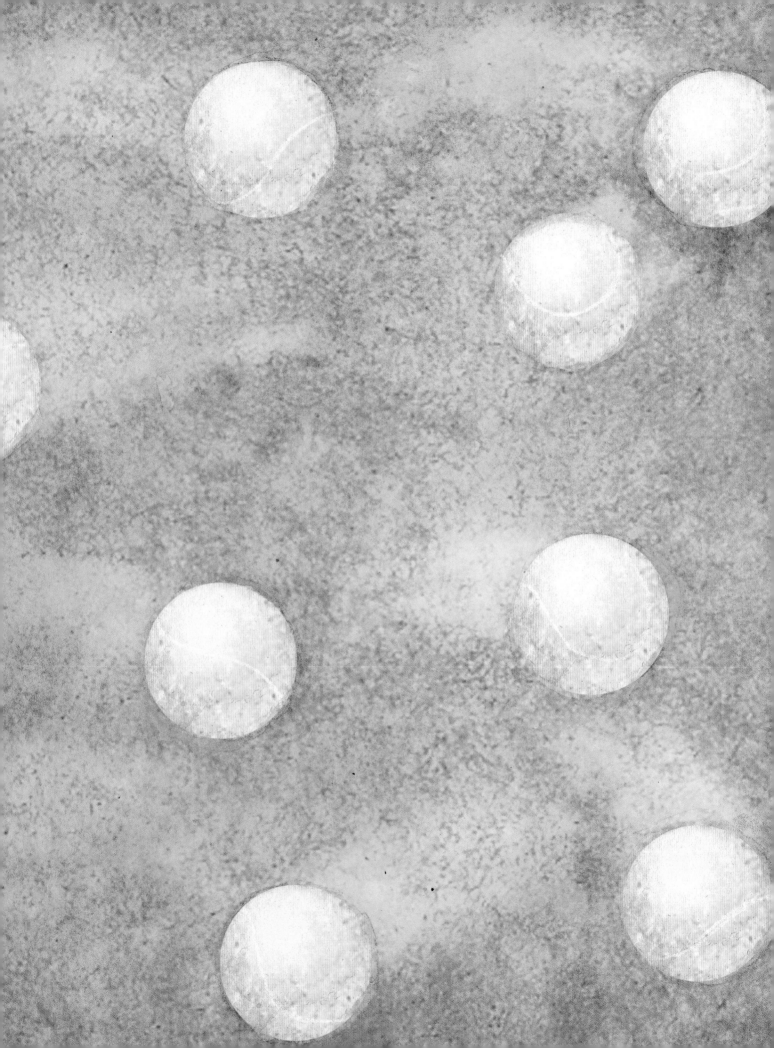

"After I beat her," Nana told the reporters, "she headed straight to the grandstand without bothering to shake my hand. Some kid had been laughing at her and she was going to throw him out. I tell you, Althea Gibson is nothing but trouble!"

It took time, a good long time, but slowly Althea learned that wanting to slug her opponent as soon as she started losing her match made her a worse tennis player than if she kept her cool.

With Buddy's help, Althea realized she could dress up in white and act like a lady, and still beat the liver and lights out of the ball.

Tennis changed Althea, all right.

But just as importantly . . .

Ever since Miss Gibson
rallied in the second set of the women's finals,
she has proven to be nothing but trouble
for seasoned U.S. and world champ
Louise Brough.

Althea changed tennis.

She did it, ladies and gentlemen!
She did it! Althea Gibson has won
the championship here at
Wimbledon's Centre Court!

With that, Althea Gibson became
the first African American, man
or woman, ever to compete in
and win the coveted Wimbledon Cup,
long considered the highest honor
in tennis.

And she never did forget the man who first
saw the Champion of the World in the
wildest tomboy in Harlem.

"Tonight is the conclusion of a long and satisfying journey.

It all started on one of New York's play streets when

Buddy Walker, a play street supervisor, said,

'Althea, I believe you could become

a good lawn tennis player.'

With those words,

he handed me my first tennis racket.

Tonight I thank Buddy Walker

for a most satisfying victory."

Author's Note

Althea Gibson was born in 1927 into a family of sharecroppers. In 1957, she became the greatest female tennis player in the world. Althea Gibson lived the American dream. But dreams aren't achieved alone. Though this is Althea's story, it is also Buddy Walker's story. When he reached out to a child who was not his own by buying her a tennis racket, Buddy set in motion all the wonderful things to come for Althea, who was always gracious about acknowledging the people who helped her turn her life around: "If I've made it," she wrote, "it's half because I was game to take a wicked amount of punishment along the way and half because there were an awful lot of people who cared enough to help me."

Buddy, Juan Serrell, and Fred Johnson were the first of many influential people—including doctors, teachers, housewives, even boxing greats Sugar Ray Robinson and Joe Louis—who helped Althea achieve her dreams.

But Althea would need even more supporters to help her fight her most insidious foe: racism. She has been called the "Jackie Robinson of tennis" because she was the first black player, man or woman, to break the color barrier and compete and win at Wimbledon.

The only way to reach a competition like Wimbledon is to be invited to play in smaller tournaments. The all-white United States Lawn Tennis Association (USLTA) effectively kept Althea out by not inviting her to tournaments. Their reason? She didn't have enough experience. But how could she get experience if she couldn't play?

When Alice Marble, an influential white tennis player, heard about Althea's predicament, she wrote an article in a tennis magazine insisting Althea be allowed to compete. Ms. Marble wrote that she would be "bitterly ashamed" if the sport to which she had devoted a good part of her life would not allow Althea to play simply because of the color of her skin. "If the field of sports has got to pave the way for all of civilization, let's do it," she wrote. "At this moment tennis is privileged to take its place among the pioneers for a true democracy."

The USLTA was publicly shamed and Althea began to receive invitations. Over the next seven years she competed and won many top tennis honors, including the Wimbledon Cup twice, in 1957 and 1958.

Althea Gibson died on September 28, 2003. If you want to read more about her in her own words, check out one of her excellent, though out-of-print, autobiographies from the library: *I Always Wanted to Be Somebody* and *So Much to Live For*. Or visit www.altheagibson.com.

Text copyright © 2007 by Sue Stauffacher
Illustrations copyright © 2007 by Greg Couch

All rights reserved. Published in the United States by Dragonfly Books,
an imprint of Random House Children's Books, a division of Random House, Inc., New York.
Originally published in hardcover in the United States by Alfred A. Knopf,
an imprint of Random House Children's Books,
a division of Random House, Inc., New York, in 2007.

Dragonfly Books with the colophon is a registered trademark of Random House, Inc.

Visit us on the Web! www.randomhouse.com/kids
Educators and librarians, for a variety of teaching tools, visit us at www.randomhouse.com/teachers

The Library of Congress has cataloged the hardcover edition of this work as follows:
Stauffacher, Sue.
Nothing but trouble : the story of Althea Gibson / by Sue Stauffacher ;
illustrated by Greg Couch.
p.   cm.
ISBN 978-0-375-83408-0 (trade) — ISBN 978-0-375-93408-7 (lib. bdg.)
(1. Gibson, Althea, 1927–2003. 2. African American women tennis players—
Biography—Juvenile literature. 3. Tennis players—United States—
Biography—Juvenile literature.)
I. Title.
GV994.G53S72 2007
796.342092—dc22
(B)
2006012605

ISBN 978-0-375-86544-2 (pbk.)

MANUFACTURED IN CHINA

17

1927

Althea Gibson
is born on a cotton farm
in Silver, South Carolina.

1930

Althea's family moves to
Harlem in New York City.

1949

Althea competes in
the United States Lawn Tennis
Association's (USLTA)
Eastern Indoor Tournament.

1947–1956

Althea wins ten straight
national women's singles
championships in the ATA.

1949

Althea enrolls in college
at Florida A&M, where she
plays on the women's
basketball team and the men's
golf team, in addition to
playing tennis.

1950

Althea reaches the women's
finals of the USLTA
National Championship
(now called the U.S. Open).

1958

Althea retires from amateur
tennis to become a singer,
a professional golf and tennis
player, and the state athletic
commissioner of New Jersey,
among other things.

1957, 1958

Althea wins the women's
USLTA National Championship.

Work Dress, Overskirt, Apron and Scarf

6. WORK DRESS, OVERSKIRT, APRON AND SCARF

Additional supplies

12″ of ⅛″-wide elastic

Pattern pieces

Use 4 A for Bodice Front
Use 4 B for Bodice Back
6 A Sleeve Top
6 B Sleeve Bottom

Dress

Follow the general cutting and stitching directions. Before gathering the top of the sleeve, gather the notched edge of the sleeve bottom; attach it to the sleeve top with right sides facing and the notches matching. Then attach the wrist elastic and complete the dress. This is a good pattern for using tiny pieces of fabric. We used different fabrics for the bodice, the skirt and the sleeve bottom. The little "puff" of the sleeve bottom takes very little fabric and gives the impression of a separate blouse peeking out from under the bodice.

Overskirt

Follow the general cutting and stitching directions, cutting the waistband ½″ longer than usual.

13

Apron

Following *Fig. 9*, cut an 8″ × 17″ rectangle for the apron and a 1″ × 20″ strip for the band and ties. Make a ½″ hem on one long edge of the apron. Turn under ¼″ twice on the short edges and topstitch. Gather the raw edge and pull up the gathers to measure 8″. Mark the center 8″ of the band; press under ¼″ on the ends and one long edge of the strip. Right sides together, matching raw edges, pin the skirt to the center of the band; stitch in place. Press the seam toward the band. Fold the band in half over the edge of the apron and topstitch along the entire strip close to the edge.

Scarf

Following *Fig. 10* for the dimensions, cut a right triangle of fabric. Narrow-hem the raw edges.

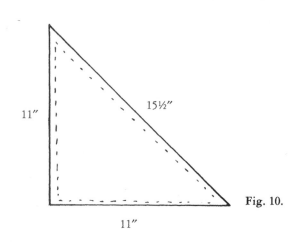

Fig. 10.

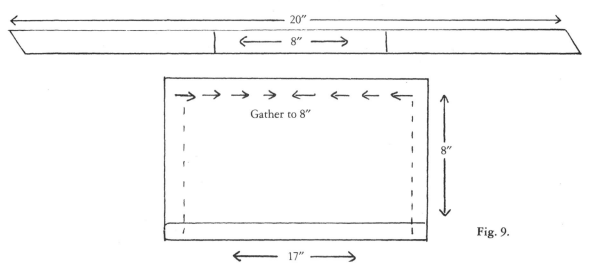

Fig. 9.

---

7. TUCKED DRESS, BONNET AND PINAFORE

Additional supplies

Four ⅛″ buttons
Snaps
Scraps of iron-on interfacing

Pattern pieces

7 A Collar
Use 4 A for Bodice Front
Use 4 B for Bodice Back
Use 4 C for Sleeve
Use 5 C for Collar Facing
7 B Bonnet
7 C Lower Bonnet Facing
7 D Bonnet Brim
7 E Pinafore Front
7 F Pinafore Back
7 G Heart Pocket
Use 2 A for Pinafore Yoke Front
Use 2 B for Pinafore Yoke Back

Dress

Cut the skirt 13½″ × 36″. Make a ½″ hem on one long edge. Starting 1¼″ above the hem, make two ½″-wide tucks, spaced 1″ apart. To trim the bodice front, cut a 1″ × 4″ strip of matching fabric. Fold under ¼″ on the long edges; press.

Topstitch the strip to the center front of the blouse to form a "placket." Attach the collar and complete the dress following the general instructions. Sew the buttons to the front "placket."

Bonnet

Iron the interfacing to the wrong side of one bonnet brim. Sew the brim pieces together along the curved edge. Clip, trim, turn and press. Press under the seam allowance on the top edge of the bonnet facing. Sew the bottom of the bonnet to the facing with the right sides together, leaving the top edge open and ending the stitching at the lower casing line. Clip and trim the seam; turn right side out and press. Topstitch across the top of the facing very close to the edge. Stitch again ¼″ away to form a casing. Gather the front edge of the bonnet as indicated. Pin the straight edge of the brim to the right side of the gathered edge of the bonnet, pulling up the gathers to fit. Stitch. Press the seam toward the bonnet. For the tie, cut a 1″ × 24″ strip of fabric. Fold the long raw edges to the center, then fold the strip in half with the right side out. Topstitch. Run the tie through the casing.

Pinafore

Cut two yoke fronts and four yoke backs. Be sure to reverse the pattern for two of the backs. One front and two backs will

14

Tucked Dress

be used for the facing. Stitch the pocket pieces together, leaving an opening to turn. Clip and trim the seam; turn right side out and press. Topstitch the pocket to the pinafore skirt front, leaving the top of the pocket open above the notches. Sew the shoulder seams of the yoke and the facing. Place the yoke, right side up, on the work surface; place the facing, wrong side up, on top of it. Stitch the neck, armhole and back edges *(Fig. 11)*. Leave ¼″ at the bottom of the yoke free to attach the skirt. Turn the piece right side out by pulling the backs through the shoulder area. This will take patience. Sew the side seams of the skirt pieces, leaving the armhole edges open. Turn in the seam allowances on the armholes and stitch. Turn in the center back edges and stitch. Gather the top edges of the skirt. Pin the skirt pieces to the yoke with the right sides together. Stitch, being careful not to catch the facing in the stitching. Turn under the bottom of the facing and blindstitch in place. Make a ½″ hem on the lower edge of the skirt.

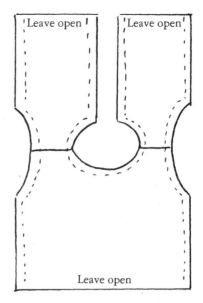

Fig. 11.

Tucked Dress with Bonnet and Pinafore

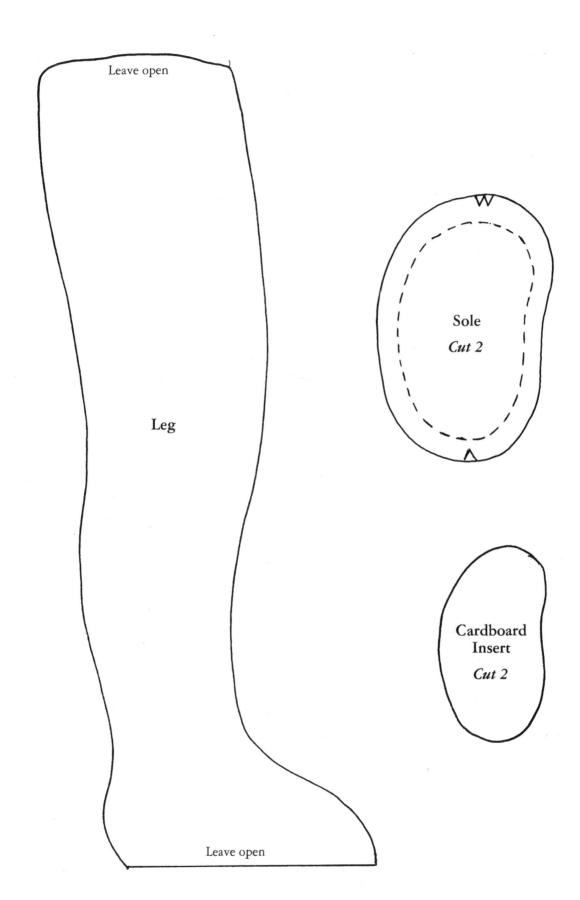

Leave open

Leg

Sole

Cut 2

Cardboard
Insert

Cut 2

Leave open

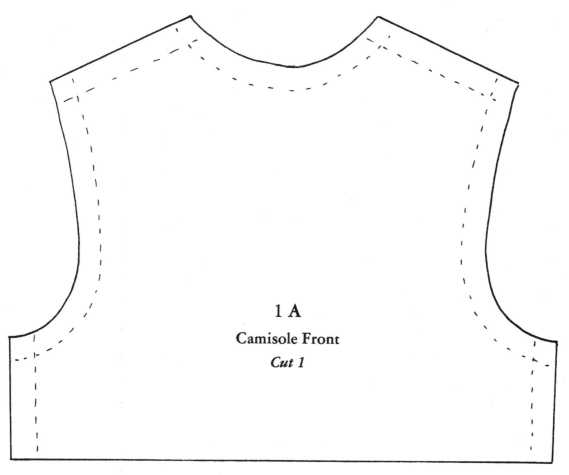

1 A

Camisole Front

Cut 1

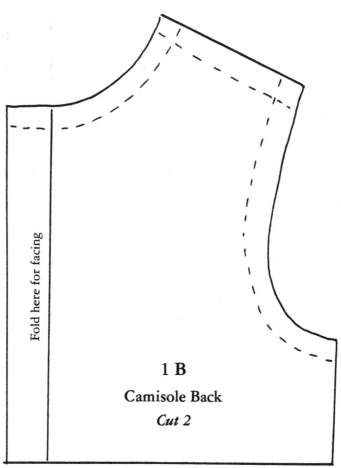

Fold here for facing

1 B

Camisole Back

Cut 2

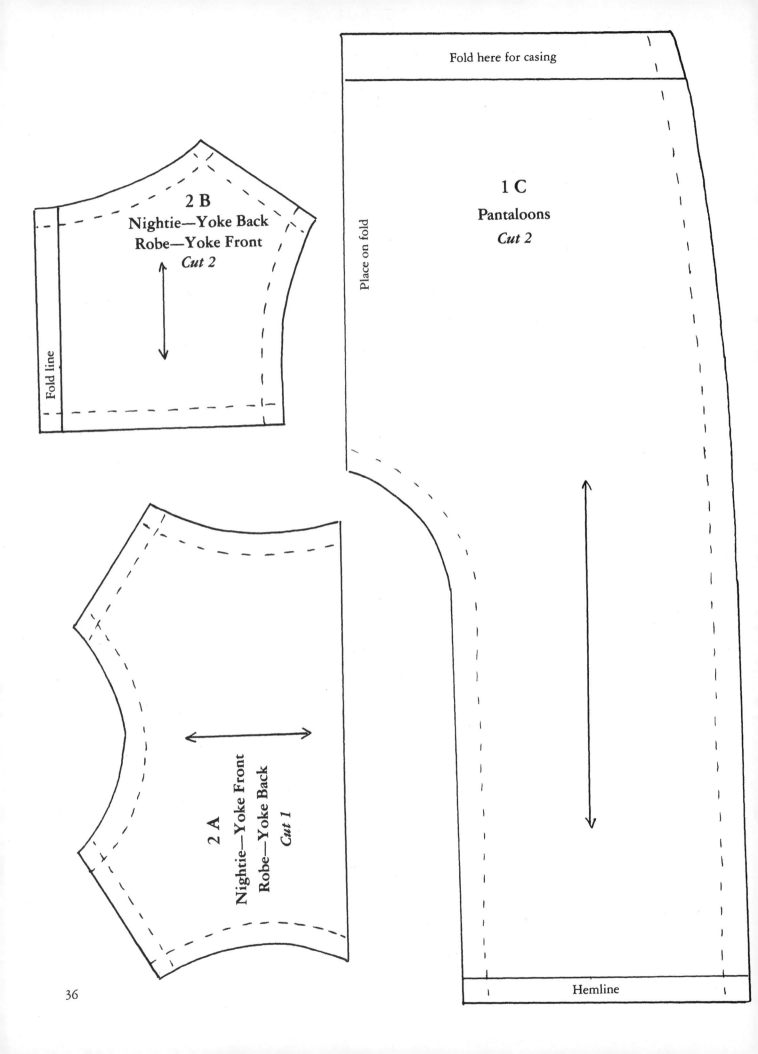

2 B
Nightie—Yoke Back
Robe—Yoke Front
Cut 2

Fold line

2 A
Nightie—Yoke Front
Robe—Yoke Back
Cut 1

Fold here for casing

1 C
Pantaloons
Cut 2

Place on fold

Hemline

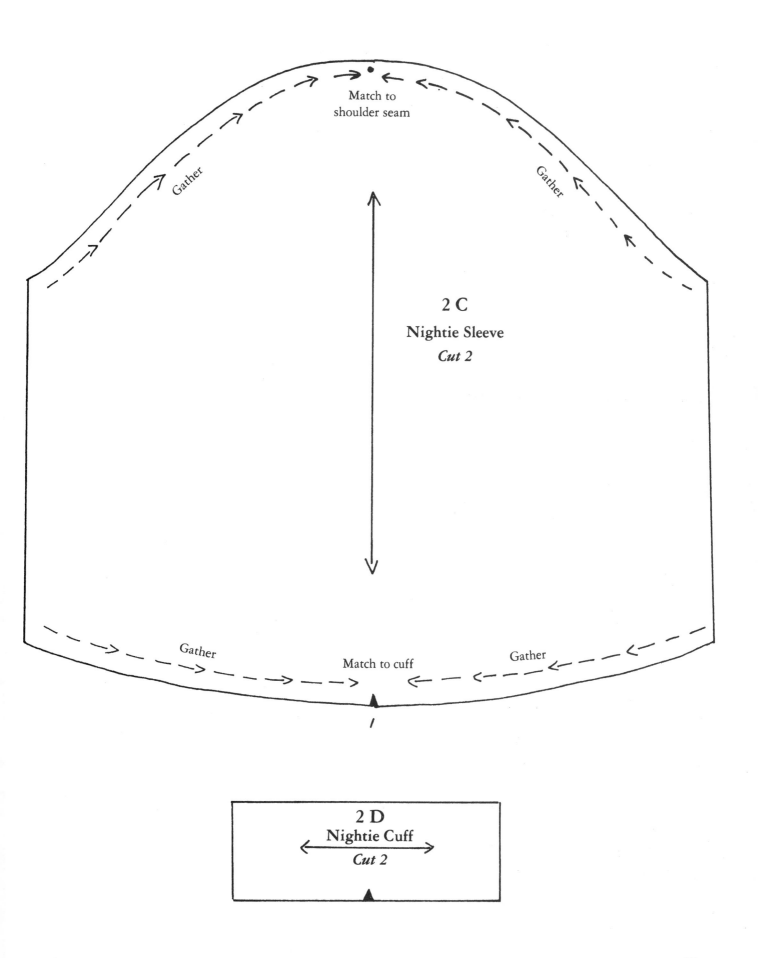

Match to
shoulder seam

Gather

Gather

2 C

Nightie Sleeve

Cut 2

Gather

Match to cuff

Gather

2 D

Nightie Cuff

Cut 2

Join the top of the pattern to the bottom of the pattern, overlapping the shaded portions.

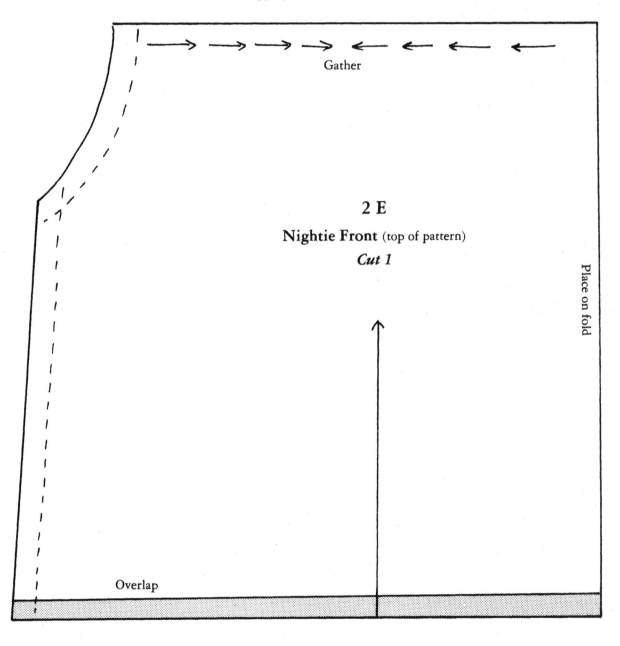

Gather

2 E

Nightie Front (top of pattern)

Cut 1

Place on fold

Overlap

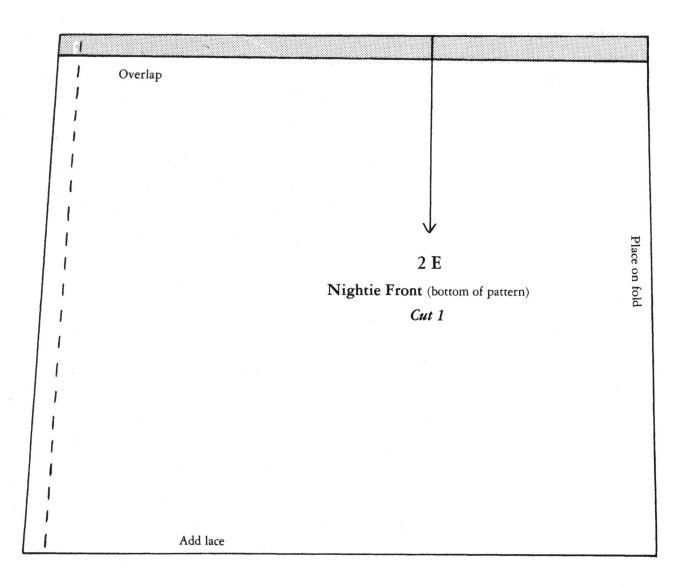

Overlap

2 E

Nightie Front (bottom of pattern)

Cut 1

Place on fold

Add lace

Join the top of the pattern to the bottom of the pattern, overlapping the shaded portions.

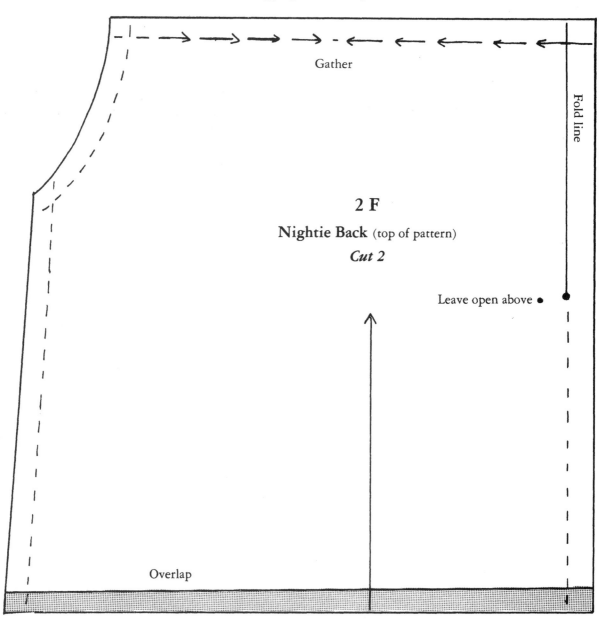

Gather

Fold line

2 F

Nightie Back (top of pattern)

Cut 2

Leave open above ●

Overlap

Overlap

2 F

Nightie Back (bottom of pattern)

Cut 2

Add lace

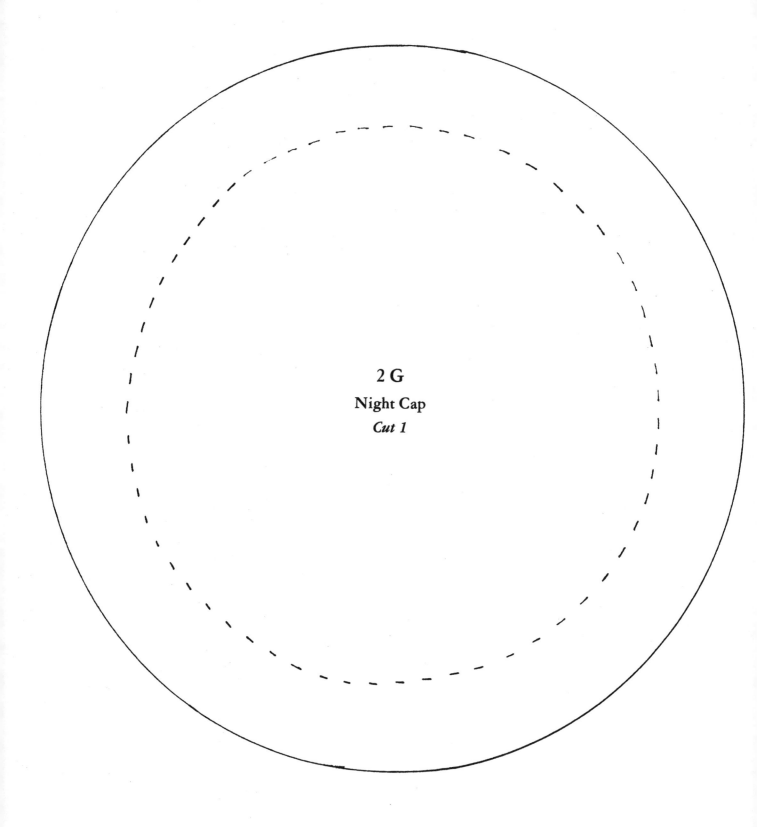

2 G
Night Cap
Cut 1

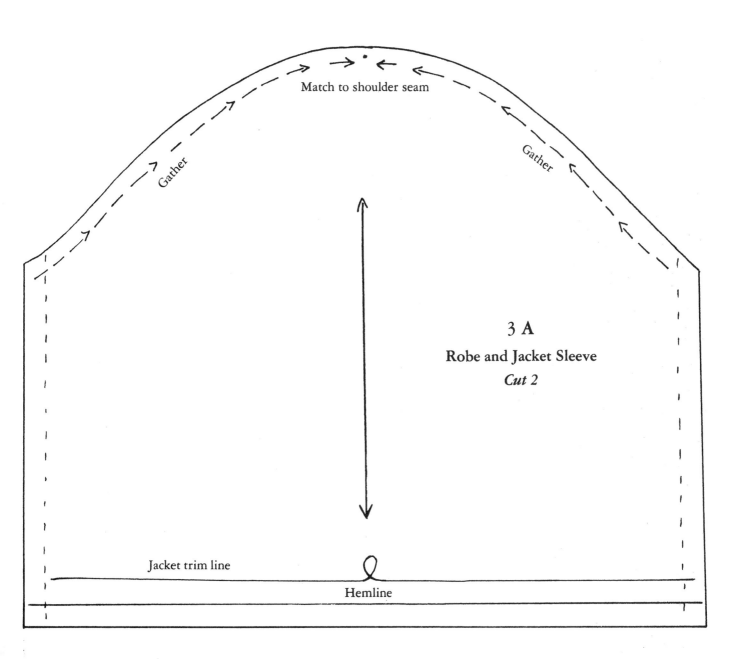

Match to shoulder seam

Gather

Gather

3 A
Robe and Jacket Sleeve
Cut 2

Jacket trim line

Hemline

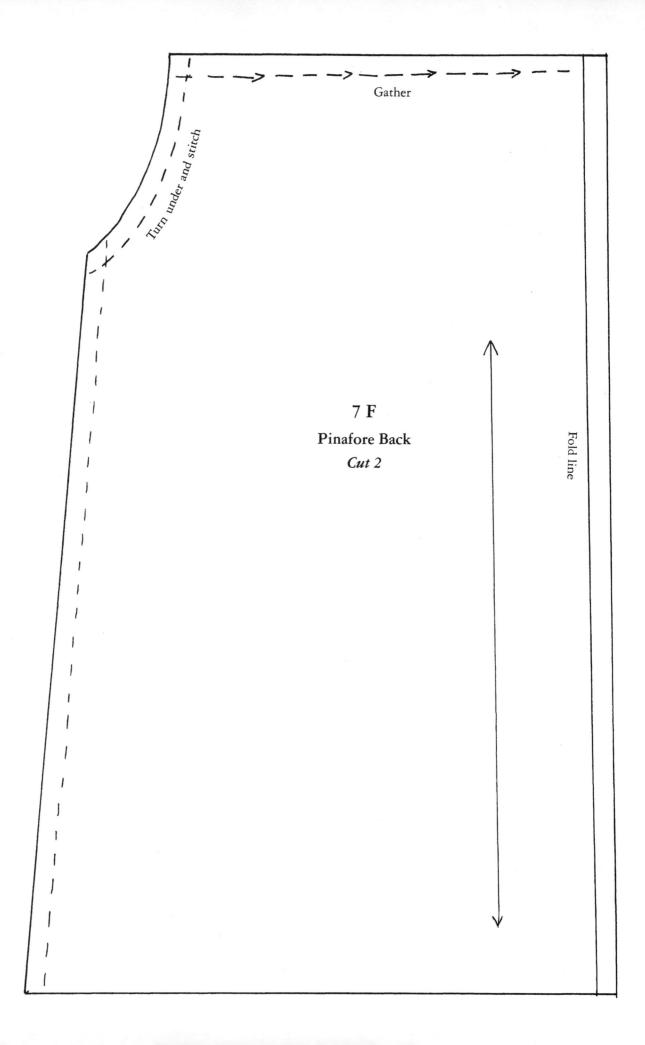

Gather

Turn under and stitch

7 F
Pinafore Back
Cut 2

Fold line

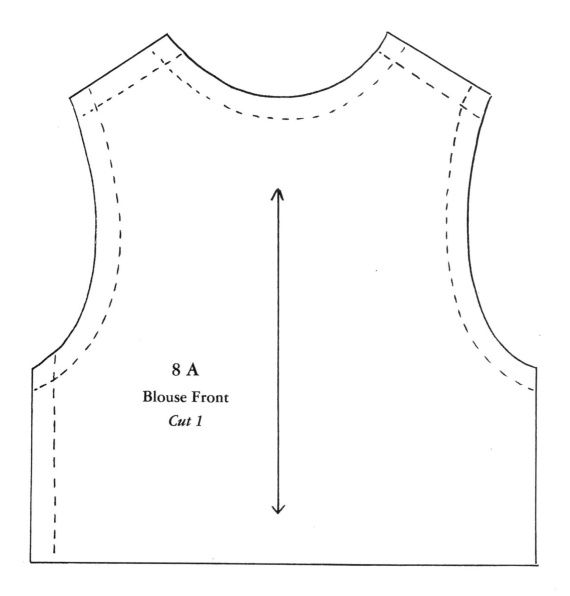

8 A

Blouse Front

Cut 1

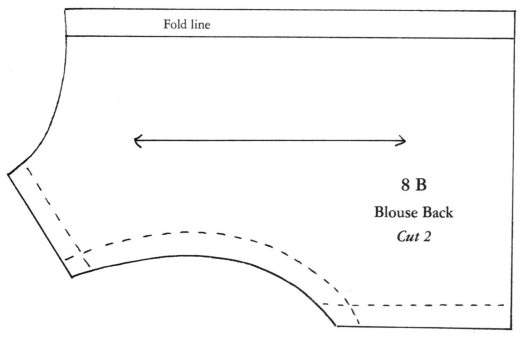

Fold line

8 B

Blouse Back

Cut 2

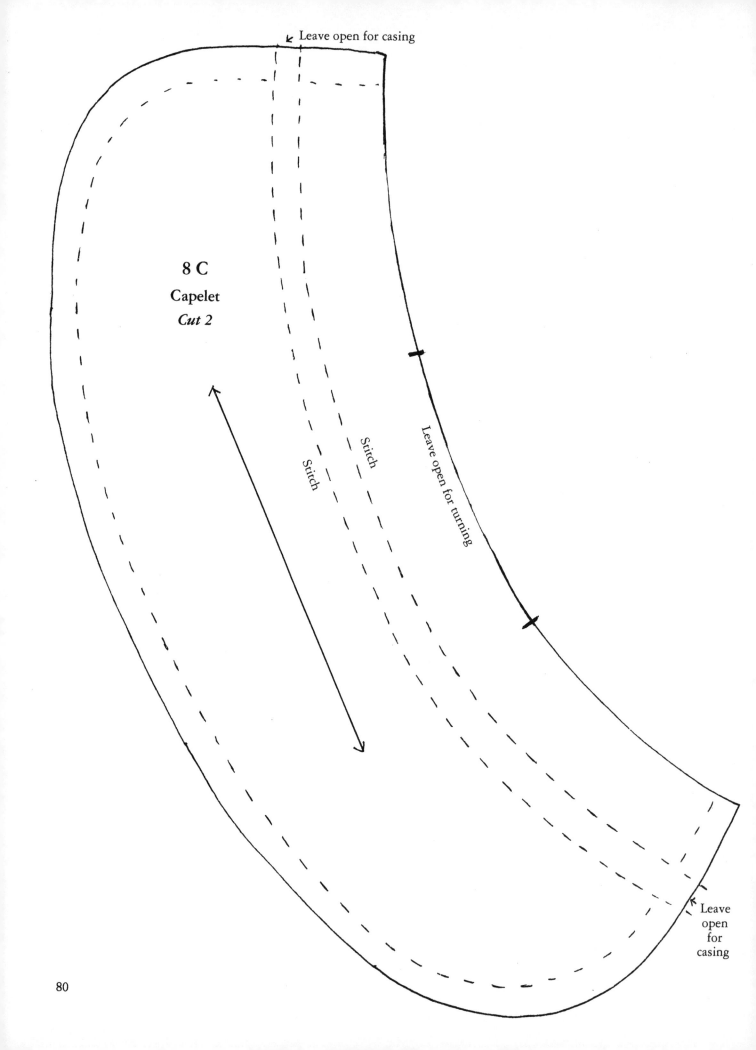

Leave open for casing

8 C
Capelet
Cut 2

Stitch

Stitch

Leave open for turning

Leave open for casing

80

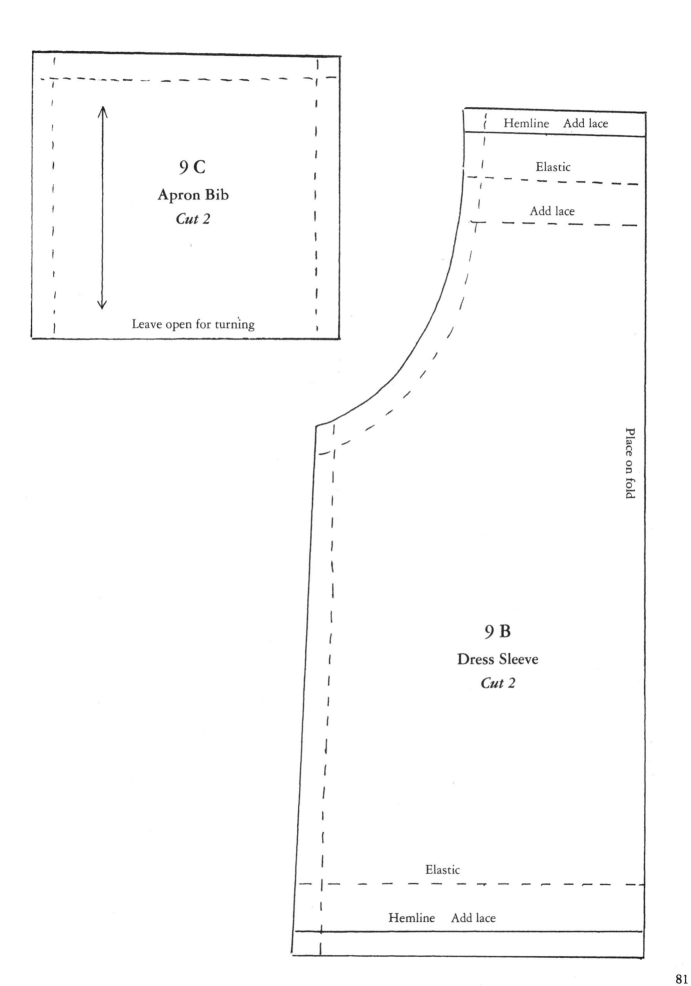

9 C
Apron Bib
Cut 2

Leave open for turning

Hemline   Add lace

Elastic

Add lace

Place on fold

9 B
Dress Sleeve
Cut 2

Elastic

Hemline   Add lace

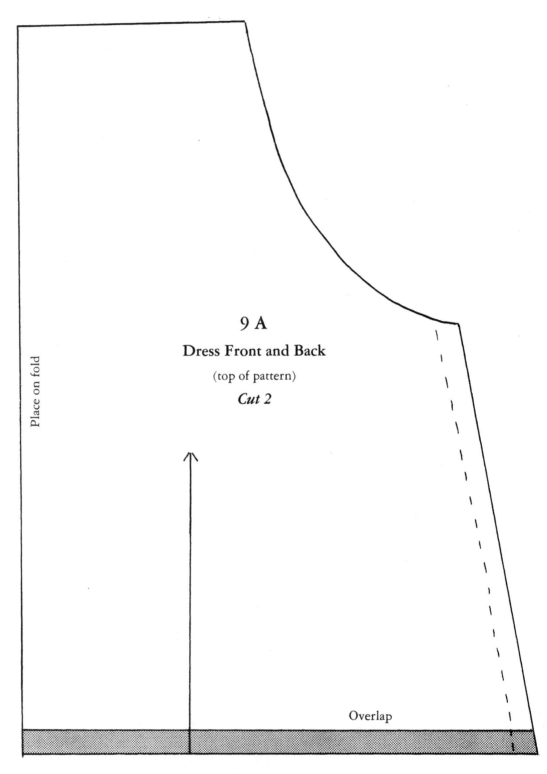

Place on fold

9 A

Dress Front and Back

(top of pattern)

Cut 2

Overlap

Join the top of the pattern to the bottom of the pattern,
overlapping the shaded portions.

Overlap

Place on fold

9 A

Dress Front and Back

(bottom of pattern)

Cut 2

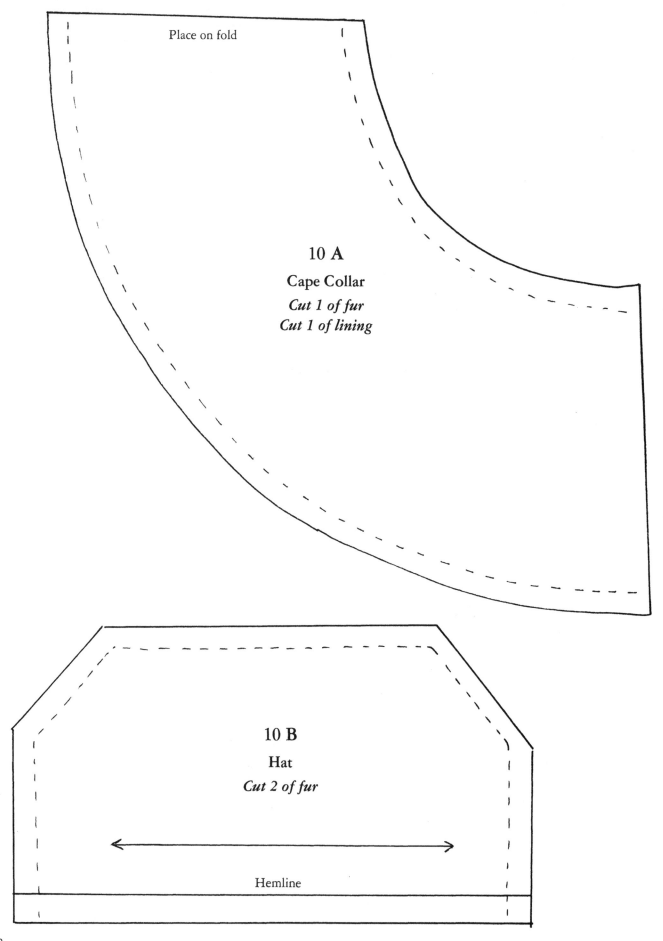

Place on fold

10 A

Cape Collar

Cut 1 of fur
Cut 1 of lining

10 B

Hat

Cut 2 of fur

Hemline

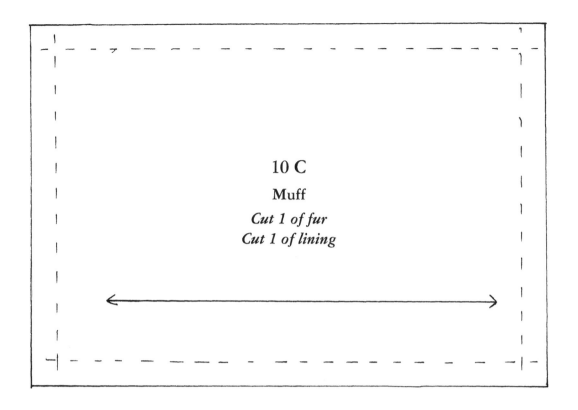

10 C

Muff

Cut 1 of fur
Cut 1 of lining

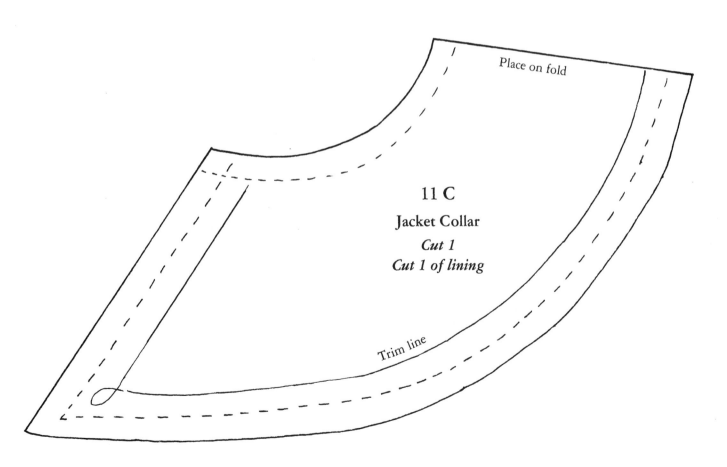

Place on fold

11 C

Jacket Collar
Cut 1
Cut 1 of lining

Trim line

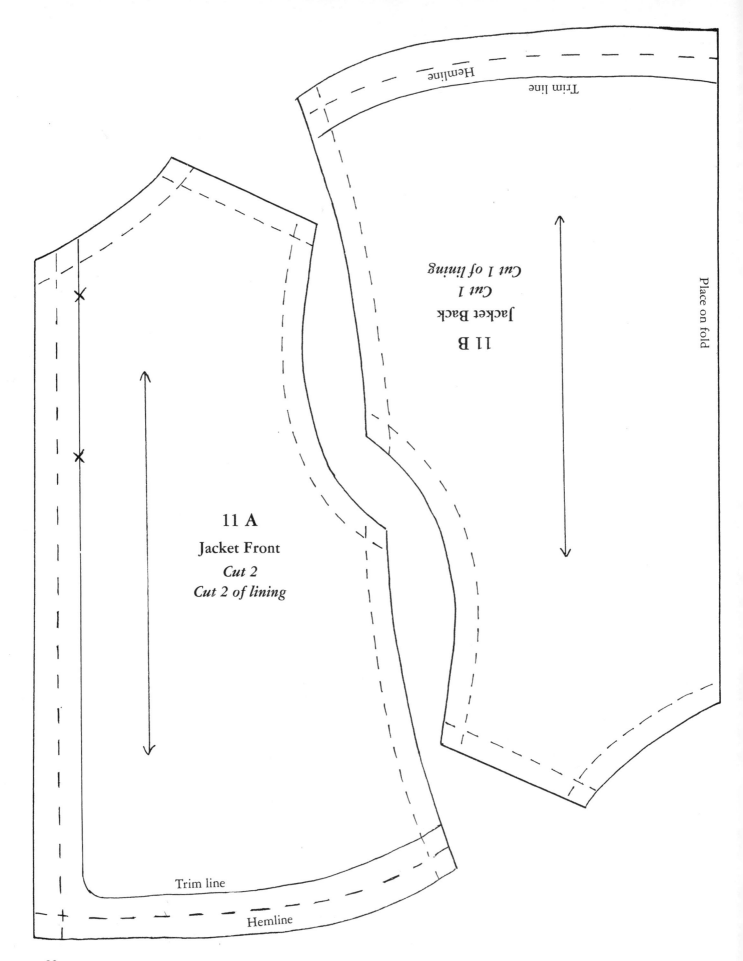

11 A

Jacket Front

Cut 2
Cut 2 of lining

Trim line

Hemline

11 B

Jacket Back
Cut 1
Cut 1 of lining

Hemline

Trim line

Place on fold

Hemline

Trim line

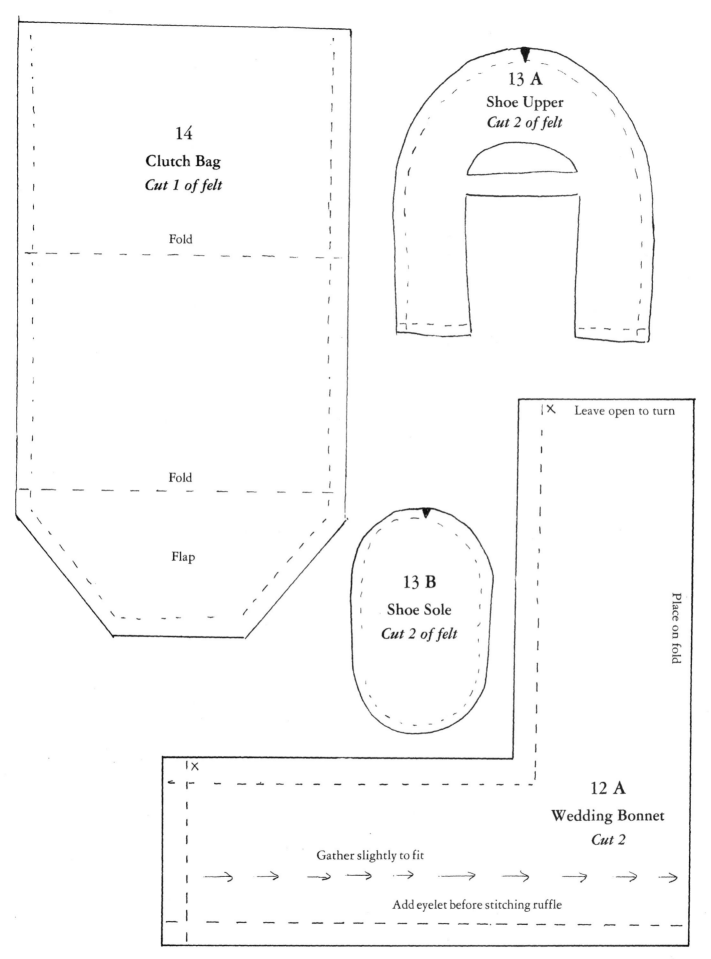

14
Clutch Bag
Cut 1 of felt

Fold

Fold

Flap

13 A
Shoe Upper
Cut 2 of felt

13 B
Shoe Sole
Cut 2 of felt

| X Leave open to turn

Place on fold

| X

12 A
Wedding Bonnet
Cut 2

Gather slightly to fit

Add eyelet before stitching ruffle